A MATERIAL WORLD

An Exhibition at the National Museum of American History

Smithsonian Institution

By Robert Friedel

Color photography by Eric F. Long

1988

This publication has been prepared in conjunction with the exhibition *A Material World* at the National Museum of American History, Smithsonian Institution. The author is grateful to all members of the exhibition team for their assistance, advice, and encouragement. Thanks are due to Amy Bix, Kenneth Arnold, Jeffrey Meikle, Steven Lubar, and Susan Tolbert for their help with particular aspects of the work. The greatest debt, however, is owed to the exhibition's coordinator, Claudine Klose, without whose skill, perseverance, and never-failing good humor, none of this would have been possible.

This publication was made possible by generous support from E.I. du Pont de Nemours and Company.

This publication is available from the
Department of Public Programs
National Museum of American History
Smithsonian Institution
Washington, D.C. 20560

FRONT COVER
Leo Baekeland with his family at his Yonkers, New York, home, surrounded by the materials of his world: wood, metal, cloth, glass, and many others.
Courtesy of the Leo Baekeland Papers, Archives Center, National Museum of American History

INSIDE FRONT COVER
The George Washington Bridge in final stages of construction
Courtesy of the The Port of New York Authority

An Appreciation

The exhibition *A Material World* is an introduction to the entire National Museum of American History. Like every large exhibition, it is a team effort to which many individuals contributed mightily. Virtually every curatorial unit, curator, specialist, and technician became involved at one time or another.

The idea of an exhibition on materials was conceived by Jon Eklund, curator in the Division of Computers, Information, and Society. In 1984 Jon and I presented this idea to Ed Jefferson, chief executive officer of E.I. du Pont de Nemours and Company in Wilmington, Delaware. Arthur Molella and William Withuhn, chairman and vice-chairman respectively of our Department of the History of Science and Technology, and Richard Woodward in Wilmington also contributed early on. In 1985 du Pont generously agreed to fund the exhibition in full.

Next came the task of transforming idea into reality. First I invited Jeff Howard to come on board as the designer. Then I contracted with the ideal team of historical consultants, Robert D. Friedel of the University of Maryland and Jeffrey Meikle of the University of Texas. Robert C. Post, curator of the exhibition, developed the concept and script in concert with those three, and with associate curator Claudine Klose. Stanley Goldberg and Michael Judd of our Division of Education worked with the curators and designer to develop the exhibition's interactive elements.

The key administrative roles were capably filled by L. Susan Tolbert of our Division of Transportation, who served as collections manager, and by Steven Lubar, project manager. Early on Ronald Becker, our assistant director for administration, and William Withuhn served important management roles as well.

Even a brief list of some of the other people who contributed to the exhibition gives an idea of the breadth of expertise demanded by an undertaking of this size and complexity. Thanks are due to Amy Bix, Karen Clifford, Bonnie Lilienfeld, Kelly Welch, and especially Kenneth Arnold for their industry as curatorial assistants; Karen Loveland and John Hiller of the Smithsonian's Office of Telecommunications, William T. Tearman of the Museum's Department of Exhibits, and consultant Benjamin W. Lawless for the audiovisual components; John Stine of our Division of Transportation for deft logistical help with the major artifacts; Martin Burke and Larry Jones of our Division of Conversation for the restoration program; Lenny Bodenlos for help as a volunteer; David Shayt of our Division of Engineering and Industry for unfailing intelligence in special curatorial assignments; Richard Nicastro, deputy assistant director for exhibits, and Robert Norton, chief of our Exhibits Production Division, for keeping the production of the exhibition on track; John Battle and Peter Maratta for the detail drawings, Marcia Powell for model making, and Wayne Poole for specifying materials applications; the team at our Silver Hill storage facility, headed by Patrick Ladden; and the Smithsonian's Office of

Printing and Photographic Services under James Wallace, especially Eric Long for the splendid photographs that appear in this book and in the exhibition.

Along the way, the curatorial-design team availed itself time and again of the special expertise of the Exhibition Advisory Committee: Dick Woodward, F. Hamilton Fish, Jr., and Herman Schroeder of du Pont, Merritt Roe Smith of the Massachusetts Institute of Technology, and Robert Kohler of the University of Pennsylvania. This committee carried the primary load of critiquing the script as it evolved over a two-year period, with valuable commentaries also provided by several others, notably Robert B. Gordon of Yale University and our curator in the Division of Engineering and Industry, Robert M. Vogel.

All museum exhibitions depend ultimately on the generosity of those who lend and donate artifacts for display. With several hundred artifacts, *A Material World* is a beneficiary of dozens of donations made in conjunction with the Museum's ongoing collecting program, and these donors are duly credited in the exhibition itself. There is a special category of donor-lender, however, those who came through *specifically* for *A Material World*, after the conceptual scheme had been refined and we stood in need of key objects to illustrate and exemplify those concepts. These donors and lenders are listed below:

Donors

Dale Armstrong
BALDT Inc.
Larry Balma
Battelle Memorial Institute
Bescar Industries
Bryden-American Co.
Castle Metals
Cencom Research Associates, Inc.
Continental Beverage Packaging, Division of Continental Can Company, Inc.
E.I. du Pont de Nemours and Company
F. Hamilton Fish, Jr.
Don Garlits Museum of Drag Racing
Empire of Carolina, Inc., Richard Nugent
Industrial Sales Corp.
Ron Kronavich, Maytag Co.
Estelle and Erwine Laverne
Lehigh University
Ralph J. Lubasco
Ludlow-Rensselaer Hydrant Co.
National Capital Parks—Central
National Hot Rod Assn.
Diane Odgers
Pencil Makers Assn.
Carmine Petito
Robert A. Podrog
Port Authority of New York and New Jersey
George Powell, The Powell Corp.
Al Prueitt and Sons, Inc.
Purdue University
Steven Smolian
SPS Technologies
Simpson Safety Products
Craig Stecyk
Super Shops, Inc.
Trow and Holden Co.
Henry Velasco
Von Fange Tool Co.

Lenders

ALCOA
Jeanne Benas
Patti Cass
Michael R. Harris
James Hurd
Christopher Klose
Arthur P. Molella
Motorola Museum, Motorola Corp.,
    Sharon Darling
Lisa Thoerle
Lloyd Thoburn
Mark E. Woolley
National Air and Space Museum,
    Smithsonian Institution
National Museum of Natural History,
    Smithsonian Institution
Armand and Barbara Winfield
William Yeingst

Funders, creators, donors—the realization of *A Material World* is due to a convergence of resources—financial, intellectual, artistic, and "material." We are very proud of the outcome.

Roger G. Kennedy

Director
National Museum of
American History

THE LATE GENERAL GERSHOM MOTT.
PHOTOGRAPHED BY J. E. SMITH.—[SEE PAGE 845.]

COLONEL THOMAS L. CASEY, GOVERNMENT ENGINEER OF
THE WASHINGTON MONUMENT.—PHOTOGRAPHED BY BELL.

THE LATE REUBEN R. SPRINGER.
PHOTOGRAPHED BY LANDY.—[SEE PAGE 845.]

B. R. Green, Civil Engineer.   Capt. G. W. Davis, Engineer.   P. H. McLaughlin, Superintendent.   Col. T. L. Casey, Government Engineer.   James Hogan, Rigger.   Lewis O'Brien (colored).

572 FEET HIGH—SETTING THE CAP-STONE ON THE WASHINGTON MONUMENT.—FROM A SKETCH ON THE SPOT BY S. H. NEALY.—[SEE PAGE 844.]

Ceremonies accompanied the setting of the aluminum apex atop the Washington Monument
on December 8, 1884, from *Harpers Weekly.*
Courtesy of the Library of Congress

Contents

Introduction

A few words about museums, artifacts, materials, and the exhibition *A Material World*

Most of us believe that objects from the past can teach, inspire, admonish, elate, amuse, and enrich us. How and why objects do this is mysterious, the sort of question that museum people occasionally ponder but which rarely bothers the rest of us. The important thing is that we almost all believe that objects from the past have this power.

Some objects are clearly more powerful than others. The power of some stems from their great age, of others from their association with great ideas, events, or people, and of still others from their evocation of sympathy or affection or dismay or horror. What we bring to objects also shapes our responses to them. For each of us, our own memories and experiences are the foundations of an object's power. Just as experiences differ from individual to individual, so will differ the responses each of us has to the objects we see and study.

The National Museum of American History contains and displays a vast number and variety of objects, ranging from postage stamps to colossal locomotives, from ancient glass to modern atomic clocks, from very common objects, like telephones, to unique national treasures, such as the Star-Spangled Banner. One of the few things that these objects (with only a handful of exceptions) have in common is that they are all artifacts—they are all made by men and women, either with their own hands or with tools and machines under their control. This is a collection not of natural objects or living things but of the artificial. These artifacts, therefore, tell us something about the people who designed, made, and used them, for they are all the products of human thought and effort. We study them in order to understand these people—our ancestors—and the world they lived in and shaped to their own purposes.

Another thing that the objects in the museum have in common—and that all artifacts share—is that they are made from something else. This fact is obvious yet anything but trivial. That everything is made from something is one of the key messages of *A Material World*, for this truism has subtle implications for how we see and understand the artifacts of our past. To comprehend an artifact and its meaning, we have to appreciate not only what it does but also where it comes from, both in form and in substance. *A Material World*, both the exhibition and this book, is intended to direct attention toward the substance of the artifacts of American history, to broaden our understanding of what makes the artifacts important for their makers and users and for us. The book roughly follows the organizational scheme of the exhibition.

A *Material World* is also about the changes in the materials that Americans have shaped and used over the last two centuries. Not only have some older materials, like steel, become much more widespread and important, but hundreds of new materials have appeared, many of them so distinctive and so widely used that the world of the late twentieth century looks and feels very different from that of our ancestors. The new metals, like aluminum and stainless steel, and the plastics and composites—ranging from celluloid to carbon-fiber reinforced resins—look and behave differently from earlier materials. They also come from different sources and so have the power to change our perception of what are and are not important natural resources or strategic commodities. The history of this change in materials is an inseparable part of the shaping of the modern technological, cultural, and political world.

Electrical switch panel largely of marble and copper used in the U.S. Capitol about 1910.

Looking at Objects and Materials

In museums and in much of daily life, we usually regard the design of an object as its most important aspect. An object's form is usually the key to its function and to understanding what we can about its maker and the world in which it was created. The material of an object, on the other hand, tells us much less about these key questions. Indeed, what an object is made of often seems to be determined by narrow constraints on what is available and appropriate. We generally pay little attention to the substance of things.

What compels us from time to time to stop and think about what an object is made of? Sometimes an object's material is unexpected or unfamiliar. Though we may not seem to pay much attention to it,

Wooden works built by Samuel Terry for a Connecticut church clock about 1830.

we all have expectations about what things are—or should be—made from. A chair made of cast iron, a flute of glass, a phonograph record of cement, or an automobile of wood all call attention to themselves because we expect these things to be made of more familiar substances. Almost everyone will wonder, "What's going on here?" in such cases. The answers are sometimes straightforward and sometimes bizarre, but they almost always tell us something about the object, its maker, and the time and place in which it was made. Learning about these things is one of the chief reasons we keep and study artifacts in the first place.

We may also study the materials in an artifact because something special has been done in transforming raw substance into finished product. This may simply be a feat of craftsmanship worthy of admiration, such as the making of a fine clock from wood or a lens from glass. Or we may recognize that the material itself is a product of human ingenuity responding to human or social needs, such as the steel that makes possible the cable for a giant bridge or the acrylic that forms the bubble of an astronaut's helmet.

What do we learn by picking an artifact apart and looking more closely at what it is made of? We get "inside" the object and begin to understand not only what it is for but also what it meant to create it, what workmanship went into it, and what transformations of nature made it possible. We get a sense of the choices made in its construction and often a clue to the values of the people who made and used it. The selection of precious substances or finely finished materials tells a different story about an artifact than the use of common or crudely made stuff. We are accustomed to make such judgments from observation of materials, but we seldom give voice to them. By stopping to explore such questions explicitly, we can come to understand better our own habits of thought as well as the complex nature of the world we have created around us.

The Brush Liberty Runabout

The automobile was not an American invention. But the transformation of what had originally been a rich man's toy into one of the most important artifacts of twentieth-century life was an American achievement. This accomplishment was the feat of a number of ambitious men working in the Midwest in the first decade of this century. Ransom Olds, the Dodge Brothers, and Henry Ford are among the first names to come to mind, but there were many less famous figures, such as Alanson P. Brush.

During a career that spanned the flourishing first decades of the American automobile industry, Brush worked as a designer for many companies, including Pontiac, Buick, and Cadillac. In 1906 Brush struck out on his own, backed by several Detroit financiers, and began producing his own runabouts—small, inexpensive cars meant, in the company's term, for "Everyman." A series of runabouts were manufactured between 1907 and 1912. At $350, the last and cheapest was the Liberty.

Others automakers of the period had identified the same broad market that Brush was aiming at—Henry Ford introduced his Model T in 1908—but the Brush was distinctive in the path it took

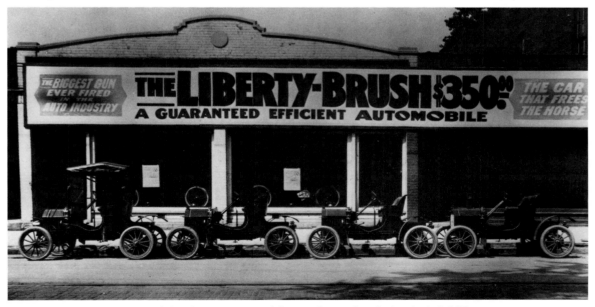

The Brush Liberty was one of the cheapest automobiles on the market during its brief life.
Courtesy of the National Automotive Historical Collection, Detroit Public Library

to affordability. Most small vehicles in the early twentieth century were made of wood, but the Brush went perhaps the furthest in attempting to adapt the easily shaped, lightweight, and familiar material to the needs of a reliable road car. Oak, hickory, and maple were used not only in the frame and wheels, but also in the axles. The motor was small, even for the time, and the car was not meant to go more than thirty miles per hour. Some Brushes used aluminum in the crankcase to save weight (the Liberty weighed only nine hundred pounds), and the cheapest model replaced the leather upholstery of other models with Pantasote—a cheap, fabric-based substitute.

The Brush was not a very reliable vehicle; its small engine and wooden construction had a hard time of it on the rough roads of the day. The route to Everyman's automobile was not to be through cheap materials and small engines, but through mechanized mass-production on an enormous scale. The Brush Runabout Company went into bankruptcy in 1912, just as Henry Ford was gearing up his new Highland Park, Michigan, factory to produce the "people's car" by the millions.

The George Washington Bridge Cable

One of the most distinctive characteristics of the technology of the twentieth century is the scale of things. We are capable of making things much bigger and much smaller than earlier generations could have imagined. This has enabled us to carry and manipulate great amounts of information in very tiny spaces; to transport through the air or over the seas many hundreds of people at once; to engineer life at the level of the single cell or even smaller; to build and live in towers rising hundreds of feet into the air. The fundamental scale that has always governed human life and work—the size of our bodies and our hands—no longer seems relevant to determining what we do or what we want to do. Nowhere is this more evident than in the structures we build, and nowhere more spectacularly than in our bridges.

When the George Washington Bridge (or Fort Lee Bridge, as it was first called) opened to connect the upper end of Manhattan Island with New Jersey in 1931, its central span was thirty-five hundred feet long—almost twice the length of the central span of any previous bridge. Since the early nineteenth century bridge builders had favored the suspension form for long spans. The work of John A. Roebling, capped by his Brooklyn Bridge of 1883, provided the basic model for the ambitious efforts of the twentieth century. Like all later bridge builders, Othmar Ammann, the chief engineer of the George Washington Bridge, was greatly influenced by Roebling's example.

Compressing the steel wire cables of the George Washington Bridge

Roebling also showed the material that would give the best results for such efforts—steel drawn and spun into giant wire cables. More than fifty years after he had chosen this material for the Brooklyn Bridge, it was still the choice for the giant bridge over the Hudson. The George Washington Bridge has four such cables, two on each side, each consisting of 26,474 cold-drawn galvanized steel wires, each 0.196 inches in diameter, compacted into a cable diameter of about 36 inches. Each wire is strong enough to support a weight of more than 7,000 pounds; to-gether they can hold 184 million pounds aloft. The cable has a strength of more than 240,000 pounds per square inch, much greater than that of almost any other metal form. Our capacity to maximize the strength of a material by giving it the proper form is what allows us to build on the giant scale of our day.

Understanding Materials

The use of any material begins with understanding how it behaves. The world offers up an enormous variety of substances, and human modification yields even more. Choosing among these materials may be simple or straightforward, or it may be the result of a complex series of tests and decisions. The final choice will reflect values and circumstances that may be economic, political, cultural, and aesthetic. But often the most basic element in the choice of a material is physical—will the substance behave as it must in order to be useful, safe, practical, attractive, or stable?

At any one time we are aware of only a small fraction of the physical qualities of a material. These qualities include density (what we usually call weight), texture, hardness, elasticity, color, tone (sound), reflectivity and opacity (light), conductivity (heat and electricity), absorbency, strength, toughness, ductility, taste, smell, brittleness, and many others. These are largely qualities that we can observe directly, and we all retain from our observations a large store of knowledge about the qualities of the substances around us. We know that iron is hard, glass is brittle, and rubber is springy, and we unconsciously use this knowledge all the time in making things or judging the qualities of objects. Experience always has been the most important basis for judging a material.

Ordinary experience, however, is limited in what it can tell us about a substance. This is particularly true when we want to know how a material will behave under extraordinary conditions, or when we want to predict accurately the range of a material's responses to stress or change. The testing of materials is an old way of getting past the limits of experience, but systematic testing, using standardized instruments and measurements, is relatively new, emerging since the Scientific Revolution of the seventeenth century.

Even more recent is the systematic study of the relationship between the physical properties of materials and their internal structures. Although some elements of material structure are obvious, such as the grain of a piece of wood, the complexity of the structure of all materials has been appreciated only during the last century. This is due in part to a scientific probing of materials, a new curiosity about what differentiates various substances and just why they have the properties they do.

Testing

In engineering, strength, not structure, is often the primary and immediate concern. Will a beam, rod, plate, or any other form be adequate and safe for the loads and stresses it will bear? At what point will a particular piece of iron or wood or ceramic be crushed by a load or burst by steam pressure or broken by impact? For

The Riehlé Standard U.S. Screw-Power Testing
Machine, patented 1889

centuries builders and artisans answered such questions largely by experience, and if they tried something new the experiment could sometimes be costly or even tragic. By the nineteenth century, however, the impetus to build structures, design machines, and manufacture engines that were new, larger, and better overwhelmed conservative traditions. New structures and machines were almost invariably expensive. The ever-growing cost of failure—in money and, sometimes, in human lives—made it more important than ever to understand the strength and capacity of materials before they were incorporated into a building, container, or machine.

The systematic testing of structural materials was the product of the rapid growth of technology in the early nineteenth century. Special urgency was given to such testing in the United States by the problem of boiler explosions aboard steamboats, which claimed dozens of lives every year on American waterways. The use of high steam pressures in boilers of poorly made iron plate was a leading cause of explosions. The coming of the railroad and the steam locomotive in the 1830s and 1840s provided all the more reason to make the testing of materials systematic and reliable.

The universal testing machine was one of a number of devices introduced to make the testing of materials simple and dependable. The machine was called "universal" because it tested material specimens for strength in tension, in compression, and in bending (or "flexure"). By the end of the nineteenth century such machines had grown in size and power as engineers sought to test larger and larger loads. The firm of Riehlé Brothers, in Philadelphia, was one of two producers of testing machines in the United States. In 1893 the company made the largest testing machine ever built and displayed it at the World's Fair in Chicago. The machine was then bought by Purdue University in Lafayette, Indiana, where it was used in the mechanical engineering laboratories until being donated to the Smithsonian. In the Riehlé machine, giant screws apply enormous forces (up to 300,000 pounds) to either pull apart or crush a material specimen. A weighing beam at one side measures the force precisely.

Structure & Microstructure

It is the great prerogative of Mankind above other Creatures, that we are not only to behold the works of Nature, or barely to sustein our lives by them, but we have also the power of considering, comparing, altering, assisting, and improving them to various uses. . . . By the addition of such artificial Instruments and methods, there may be, in some manner, a reparation made for the mischiefs, and imperfection, mankind has drawn upon it self, by negligence, and intemperance, and a wilful and superstitious deserting the Prescripts and Rules of Nature, whereby every man, both from a deriv'd corruption, innate and born within him, and from his breeding and converse with men, is very subject to slip into all sorts of errors.

—Robert Hooke, Preface, *Micrographia* (1665)

Few distinctions in our view of nature are older than that between substance and form. All things clearly possess both, and the creation of any object involves both substance and design. Since the seventeenth century we have slowly come to understand that matter itself has form or structure. This knowledge is one of the key contributions of modern science to the understanding and use of materials. The significant levels of structure range from the atomic (or even subatomic) level of electrons and nuclei to the visible one of crystals, large cells, and layers or strata. To an important extent, the properties of all materials are defined and determined at these structural levels.

In no material is structure more visibly linked to behavior than in wood. The worker in wood has always been sensitive to the material's grain, for the strength,

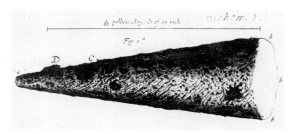

Drawing of the tip of a needle, magnified about 50 times, from *Micrographia* by Robert Hooke, 1665

flexibility, and stability of any wooden object is closely related to its orientation with or against the grain. Good woodworkers take into account structural imperfections, such as knots, cracks, and swellings before choosing a piece of wood. The visible structure of wood is also a fundamental element in its aesthetic value. A woodworker might choose the complex graining of walnut or oak for one object, the uniform appearance of birch or maple for another.

The high visibility of wood's structure is unusual. For most substances the naked eye sees a largely uniform mass, and variations in that mass seem to be mere imperfections. Such appearances, of course, are illusory. To see complexity in seeming simplicity all we need is the right instrument—most likely a microscope. This lesson, so important for modern materials science, was actually learned by the first generation of microscopists. The very first observation that Robert Hooke described in his 1665 work, *Micrographia*, was "the Point of a sharp small Needle," and nothing could have been more striking than the roughness and imperfections that showed themselves "in the Glass." Seeing more than imperfections in metals, however, was hardly possible before the nine-

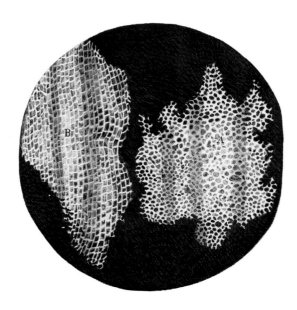

Drawing of cork, magnified about 40 times, from *Micrographia* by Robert Hooke, 1665

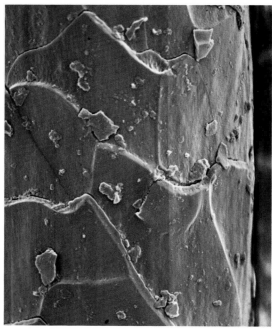

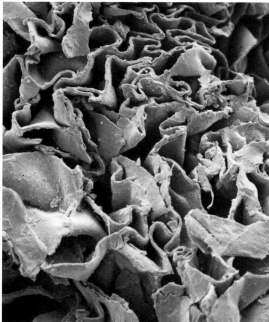

Electron micrograph of wool fibers magnified 25,
200, and 1,600 times
*Courtesy of Melanie Feather, Conservation Analytical
Laboratory, Smithsonian Institution*

Electron micrograph of cork magnified 1,000 times
*Courtesy of Melanie Feather, Conservation Analytical
Laboratory, Smithsonian Institution*

teenth century, for the microstructures of such materials can be studied only when the surfaces have been polished and then etched, a technique not really understood until the pioneering work of Henry Sorby in the 1860s.

From Sorby's studies emerged metallography—the systematic investigation of metallic microstructures. Metallographers see and record the complex mixture of crystals that characterizes all metals. The behavior of a metal often depends upon the size and shape of its crystals, the different kinds of crystals existing side-by-side (especially important in alloys), and the mixture of crystalline regions in the larger solid. Many of the ancient techniques for altering the properties of metals—tempering, quenching, annealing, cold-working, and others—are really ways of altering the distribution and proportion of the different crystals in a metal. This was not understood until the twentieth century, but our knowledge of metallography now allows us to tell just how objects in the past were made by studying their telltale microstructures.

The microscope, magnifying tens or hundreds of times, can reveal much of interest and importance in a material's structure, but much remains beyond its reach. New instruments of the twentieth century go beyond these limits, and they show levels upon levels of structure, not only in metals but in other materials, both organic and mineral. Modern techniques include the use of X rays (for studying the internal structure of crystals), of ionization (for detecting and studying very tiny quantities), and, most spectacularly, of electron beams. The first electron microscopes were demonstrated in 1931, but it took years of experimenting to find how to make the best use of the several different types. The magnification of electron microscopes is measured in the thousands and tens of thousands, and they can provide images of structures made of only a few atoms or molecules. With an electron microscope, scientists can study and compare materials with even tinier microstructures than the metals, such as ceramics. The new levels of structure revealed by these instruments also provide new glimpses of the beauty of nature's own harmonies and complexities.

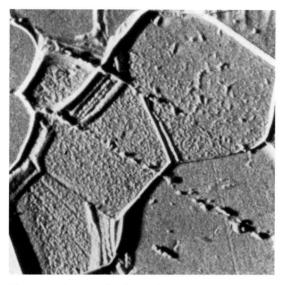

Electron micrograph of iron harpsichord wire magnified about 1,480 times
Courtesy of Dr. Robert M. Fisher, from The Metallurgy of 17th- and 18th-Century Music Wire *by Martha Goodway and Jay Scott Odell*

19

This eighteenth-century spinning wheel illustrates
the prevalence of wood in all preindustrial
mechanisms.

20

A Materials Panorama

Throughout their history, Americans have used a great variety of materials to make things. If we look carefully, we can see patterns of change in these things and in the materials that make them up. These changes have occurred for many reasons. Changing resources have meant that a material that was cheap and plentiful at one time later became scarcer, more expensive, and hence more likely to be replaced by some other material. The discovery of new sources of raw materials or new processes for extracting them has from time to time caused one substance to increase in popularity at the expense of others. The invention of new industrial or manufacturing processes or the discovery of novel materials and combinations of materials have often led to major changes in how things are made and even what they are used for or who uses them. Changing tastes and fashions have also influenced the use of materials, for materials can be as much subject to whims and styles as the designs of objects.

A careful look at the history of things American over the last two centuries reveals three roughly defined periods of materials usage that reflect not only changing materials but also changing values and patterns of life.

In the beginning there was stability—a material tradition that stretched back into the centuries when Native Americans held sway over the continent. This era continued through the decades when the United States was an agricultural nation, thriving largely on its abundance of natural re-

sources. The key materials were natural substances—useful with little alteration or preparation. Wood is the obvious example, but a host of other substances, many of them used in ways that had changed little over hundreds or even thousands of years, held important places in this traditional world: clay, straw, stone, leather, bone, horn, and many other products of nature's bounty. These materials symbolized the dominant place of the home and farm in early American life.

Hard rubber (vulcanite or ebonite) was one of the first plastics, as shown in this mid-nineteenth-century mirror.

In the early nineteenth century the United States began the long and dramatic process of industrialization. The materials central to this process were not the natural materials of tradition but the manufactured materials more suitable to factories and forges. For much of history artisans and craftsmen had supplemented the common, natural substances around them with materials that existed rarely, if at all, in usable form in nature but required the manipulation of raw materials and energy to produce and use. The metals were the most important of this class of materials, but other examples included glasses, high-temperature ceramics, and rubber. The "engines of change" that powered the Industrial Revolution—steam engines, locomotives, machine tools, and the like—were made more and more of metal, particularly iron and, later, steel. New processes, building techniques, and forms of energy (like electricity) gave increased importance to all of the manufactured materials and called forth novel ones, like rubber and aluminum, that represented the central place of advanced technology in American life.

In our own century the importance of novel materials has become even greater, marked by the emergence of a new class of substances, synthesized through chemical processing and completely unknown in nature. The synthetic materials have replaced older substances in many uses and have made possible entirely new activities, from ping pong to space travel. The most prominent of the synthetic materials are the plastics—a vast class of organic chemical combinations that combine such properties as elasticity, transparency, moldability, water- and chemical-resistance, and light weight in ways often rare or unknown in nature. Joining the plastics are advanced forms of glass and ceramics, exotic and complex alloys, and composite materials like fiberglass and Formica that combine substances in precise ways to fulfill special needs. A distinctive feature of almost all of these materials is their debt to modern chemical and materials science. Unlike the stuff of the past, these synthetics are conscious creations of human design and ingenuity, owing more to a fundamental understanding of the possibilities of nature than to accumulated experience. The bright, colorful materials of our time remind us not only of the key place of science in twentieth-century culture but also of the marvelous expansion of leisure, travel, and entertainment in this century of the common man.

Early wooden nineteenth-century candleholder

22

Natural Materials

Before the mid-nineteenth century the life of a predominantly agricultural society was reflected in the natural substances of which most things were made. This was America's wooden age.

Wood remains a key material—the source of paper, cellulose products, and chemicals as well as being used itself for building and fabricating things. Its central role is due both to its ready availability and familiarity and to its enormous variety. In a sense wood is not a material—oak, maple, walnut, pine, mahogany are materials, all with differences in strength, color, finish, hardness, and other qualities that make each more appropriate than another for various uses. Many wooden objects are as complex and subtle in their combination of materials as more obviously complicated artifacts. Traditional chairs might contain as many as a dozen different woods, selected and fitted together to take advantage of differences in wearing, swelling, aging, and other properties; even a three-piece fishing rod might have a handle of ash, a supple middle of hickory, and bamboo at the end.

In the eastern half of the United States, settlers found vast forests that were both impediments to travel, farming, and settlement and at the same time storehouses of valuable materials for the building of homes and barns, the construction of fences, tools, and wagons, and the extraction of pitch and tar. The preparation and working of wood were the most common and basic of crafts, skills not only of specialized carpenters and joiners but possessed in some measure by every farmer and tinkerer.

The wooden artifacts of preindustrial America reflect the breadth of craft skills that were applied to this material as well as wood's significance for a largely agrarian society. Farm tools like hay rakes, flails, and pitchforks were not finely finished, for they were seen as purely utilitarian implements. They were not thought likely to endure many years of hard use nor to be of much interest to anyone other than their user, who was also likely to be their maker. More complex wooden devices, such as the textile implements—wheels, reels, looms, frames, and the like—were often crafted by a specialist, or at least a particularly skilled woodworker in the neighborhood. They reveal a bit more finish and a more sophisticated use of tools in their construction, as well as a more refined sense of the possibilities of their materials. Wooden implements such as these were still primarily devices of the home, used by both women and men first to make the clothing and linen needed by a family and a productive farm and only afterwards to make products to sell.

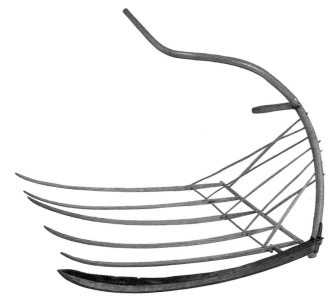

This nineteenth-century grain cradle combines flexible ash in the "fingers" with tough hickory in the "braces" to produce a sturdy harvesting tool.

Wood was the primary material of self-sufficiency, and its ease of preparation and working meant that almost every man that worked with his hands felt comfortable with it. People also admired the finer possibilities of wood, and unusually skilled craftsman were appreciated and rewarded by reputation and income. Makers of chairs and other pieces of furniture, often imitating and adapting the latest English or Continental styles, made a place for themselves in the larger towns of the colonies and the new nation. Some of their products are still treasured furnishings, carrying their names and their reputations many generations. The American environment, however, proved fertile ground for a more anonymous type of fine craftsmanship, likewise prized in our own day. The German settlements of Pennsylvania, for example, produced wooden furniture with a distinctive style and quality that combined Old World peasant traditions with the resources and values of a prosperous agrarian republic.

Wood was the material of tradition, but it also beckoned to innovators. As America began to industrialize in the late eighteenth and early nineteenth centuries, its craftsmen shaped their most familiar material into the machines and tools needed for an expanding economy. America's first factories were powered by wooden water wheels that drove wooden spinning machines, looms, and lathes. Occasionally the versatility of wood and wooden machinery was displayed to a special degree by ingenious workmen, such as Samuel Terry of Plymouth, Connecticut. Terry constructed his 1830 tower clock mechanism of black cherry, boxwood, and laurel. It represented an important tradition in American clockmaking, where careful craftsmanship and skillful use of the right woods could produce a large wooden clock about as durable and reliable as brass at only a fraction of the cost.

Although in quantity and versatility wood was clearly the key material in early America, many other natural materials made up the fabric of everyday life. The farm—home and workplace for most Americans—offered a host of substances, from the leather that provided flexible and durable coverings, containers, and belting to various fibers, such as cotton, linen, straw, and wool. These enabled many families to be practically self-sufficient in providing shoes, clothing, sacking, and the like. Even when farmers called on an itinerant craftsman to make the finished product, such as a saddle, the materials might be supplied to him from his customer's produce.

Paradoxically, one substance was the most fragile and yet most durable of early American materials—clay. Few artifacts seem more representative of an archaeologist's "dig" than fragments of pottery, clay pipe, and occasional glass or fine porcelain. And yet, of course, whole finished pieces of these materials from the seventeenth or eighteenth centuries are precious indeed. The fragments tell us how important and widespread pottery was, though we can be misled by the absence of artifacts that have long since rotted away. Straw baskets, wooden bowls and buckets, and horn or leather cups performed many of the same functions as fired or unfired clay but have left almost no telltale fragments of their existence.

Many parts of the 1912 Brush Liberty Runabout
were made of wood, even the axles.

Manufactured Materials

This safe lock from the mid-1870s used nickel-plated steel.

As America industrialized in the nineteenth century, the new place of factory and shop in national life could be seen in the new role of materials that were substantially altered as they were made or refined—especially metals, such as iron and steel, but also others, such as rubber and glass.

Metals have always been a measure of civilization. From the ancient Bronze Age, when the ability to manufacture and manipulate simple alloys of copper ushered in a new kind of society, to the nineteenth century's self-proclaimed Age of Steel, both the capacity and the willingness of peoples to use metals have marked them and the level of their culture. Metals are materials of permanence, tokens of faith in the future and of belief in the ultimate triumph of power and strength over na-

ture. Since ancient times metals such as copper (and its alloys bronze and brass), iron, silver, gold, lead, and tin have been used and valued for specific qualities. Copper is easily shaped, and bronze and brass are relatively hard and durable. These materials have been used for everything from lanterns and knives to the gears of clockwork and the tumblers of locks. Silver and gold, besides being much rarer than other important metals, are softer—easier to shape, but less durable in form. Their value derives also from their resistance to corrosion. Gold is the paragon of immutability, useful even when applied as a leafy-thin surface on baser metals. Lead and tin, and in more recent times nickel and zinc, are valued primarily for their role in alloys, although they can be found in many applications from pipe to plate to foil.

Of all the metals, however, none approaches iron for its significance to technology and the industrial society that grew up in America in the nineteenth century. Iron, in its three key forms—cast, wrought, and steel—provided the sinews for the muscle power of steam and, later, for that of electricity and internal combustion. The new forms of energy, the new machines, the new means of transport, commerce, and war that emerged in industrial America would have been unthinkable without iron.

By the time the Industrial Revolution came to America in the early nineteenth century, the basic forms of iron and how to make them were well known, even if the chemistry involved was hardly understood at all. Wrought iron, consisting of practically pure metal, was the most widely used kind. Most wrought iron was made from cast, or "pig," iron, the product of the blast furnace. In such a furnace iron ore was heated together with charcoal; the charcoal's carbon served as both

a fuel and as a chemical to assist in removing oxygen from the ore. In this process some carbon was integrated into the metallic iron, yielding a product ranging typically from 2 to 5 percent carbon. The carbon dramatically lowered the melting point of the mixture (hence it is "cast" iron), but it also made it much more brittle than pure ("malleable") iron. Cast iron could be used directly for objects needing little strength, such as pots or skillets, but most of it was laboriously reheated and beaten at a forge to rid it of carbon and make wrought iron. By the end of the eighteenth century new processes for purifying, or "converting," pig iron in larger quantities had been introduced, most notably the puddling process of Englishman Henry Cort. This process used high-temperature furnaces to burn off the carbon. The British led the way in producing and using cheaper iron, assisted by the substitution of coke (made from coal) for the increasingly scarce charcoal.

Americans were slower to make wide use of the new processes. Their forests were still abundant sources of charcoal, their coal did not make very good coke, and their wood supplies were as widespread as their forests. The first machines in America's factories were largely wood, metal was reserved for gears, bearings, spindles, and other small, easily worn parts. Traditional wood frames and joints were quite adequate for most purposes, even in advanced machinery. There were, of course, many items in the trades and the home customarily made of iron. The blacksmith supplied the farmer with the edge of the plow, the blade of the scythe, and the teeth of the harrow, just as he provided shoes and harness fittings for the

Sleigh bells from the nineteenth century combine leather and brass.

27

When stainless steel became widely available in the late 1920s, it was valued for its aesthetic possibilities as well as its technical qualities, as shown in these canape plates.

horses, andirons and spits to go into the fireplace, and nails for all kinds of construction. Even the most self-sufficient pioneer household normally relied on the blades, wire, and rods purchased (or bartered) from the local smith or brought from town out to the frontier.

One other piece of iron held a central place for many a pioneer settler—his gun. Gunsmiths usually crafted their products carefully, one at a time. Dissatisfaction with this way of doing things led to some of the most important early American experiments in mass production. The success of these experiments sprang from two technological developments: the ability to adapt metalworking to machines and the production of iron of such consistent quality and in such standard forms that machines could work piece after piece with little or no adjustment. Machine tools—lathes, milling machines, presses,

punches, and the like—were devised and improved as nineteenth-century industrialization continued. More and more these machine tools came to be made entirely of iron, embodying in their form and substance the material at the heart of the emerging machine civilization.

The most difficult form of iron to make is steel, for in steel the amount of carbon must be kept in careful balance between the relatively large quantity (2 to 5 percent) in cast iron and the negligible amount (less than half a percent) in malleable iron. Before the mid-nineteenth century and the recognition of the real role of carbon, steel makers achieved this balance only at the cost of much time, skill, and fuel. Although steel was appreciated for its superiority in holding an edge, in

Desk lamp of Bakelite and aluminum, designed by W. D. Teague about 1940

This "American Beauty" iron combines Bakelite, chrome, and stainless steel to transform a workaday object into a striking sculpture.

maintaining strength without brittleness, and in its workability, it was used for only a few things, such as the blades of knives, razors, and swords, springs for watches and for carriages, and fine wire used in pianos and scientific instruments. All of this changed, however, in the second half of the nineteenth century. In England, Henry Bessemer and, independently in America, William Kelly, announced in 1856 a method of making steel "without fuel." In the following decades their process of blowing air through molten pig iron to burn out the carbon was followed by other inexpensive methods, notably the open-hearth furnace, which made good use of scrap metal. Steel rapidly became the primary material of the industrial world, cheap enough to use in railroads, bridges, and skyscrapers, as well as in road signs, food cans, and bicycle wheels.

The new processes helped to remake the American technological environment in the second half of the nineteenth century. Industrialists (Andrew Carnegie, for example) made great new fortunes as the quantity of steel used in all parts of life exploded. In 1870 American steel producers made less than fifty thousand tons; twenty years later, they made almost five million tons; after another thirty years, total American production was close to fifty million tons. This figure for 1920 represented 59 percent of the world's steel output. Steel, more than any other material, was the instrument of American technological and economic dominance in the twentieth century.

The growth of steel appeared in many places: in railroads and shipping; in the motors, generators, and machines of the

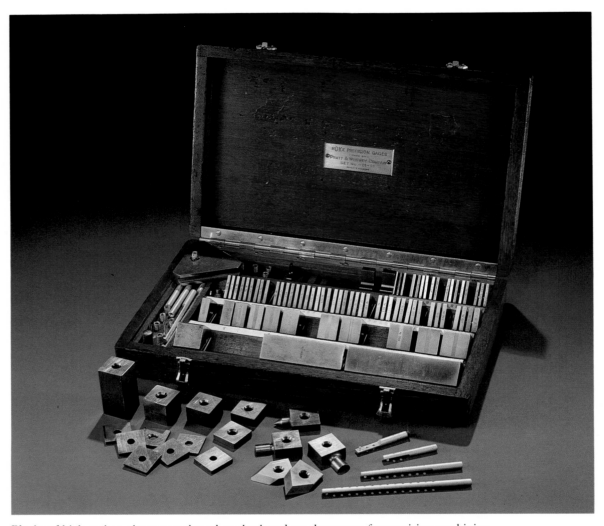

Blocks of high-carbon chrome steel used to check and set the gauges for precision machining

new electrical industry; in the beams and girders that made skyscrapers possible; and in the appliances that gradually changed the look and feel of the American home. The ease with which steel could be made into sheets, and then bent, stamped, pressed, and cut into innumerable shapes, made it the key to the mechanization of the household. The primary token of this was the refrigerator; the wood that had made up the traditional icebox was wholly unsuited for the electric refrigerator, so when smaller and quieter motors and improved design made the home refrigerator attractive in the late 1920s, it was a great steel box that came into the kitchen. This

30

was of no small importance to the steel industry. When the Great Depression struck, total steel production dropped 75 percent in three years, but refrigerator sales held their own through the 1930s. Other appliances, such as washing machines, followed, and great steel boxes became an accepted part of everyday life.

Other metals played crucial roles in industrializing America. The most important of these were copper (and its alloys) and aluminum. Copper has traditionally been the second most important metal, and its production and use expanded enormously in the nineteenth century. Besides being important in a wide range of manufactured goods, from steam engines to pins, copper was essential to the growth of the electrical industry, first in the ex-

The interior of the Maytag "Master" washing machine shows advanced materials such as aluminum and synthetic resins.

panding telegraph network at mid-century and then in even greater quantities in the electric power systems that sprang up everywhere in the 1880s and 1890s. New sources of supply were just as important to copper's expansion as accelerating demand. First in the upper Great Lakes and then in the Far West, Americans exploited huge newfound lodes of copper ore. Mining companies began to tap the high-quality deposits on the shores of Lake Superior in the 1840s, and the millions of tons of ore drawn from the region transformed the world's copper industry. The colossal mines that opened up in Montana, Utah, and Arizona toward the end of the century had even greater impact. New techniques allowed the removal of entire mountains of low-grade ore, giving the electrical networks just what they needed to continue their expansion.

Electricity was also a central part of aluminum's story, not so much as a source of demand, but as the central tool for making the metal itself. Metallic aluminum is unknown in nature. Its existence was hardly suspected before the nineteenth century. But by century's end a process that used electricity to make the metal in great quantity and purity became the basis of a growing industry. Because aluminum was so new and different, it took several decades to establish its uses and to make it the common material it is today, found in everything from foil and cans to the sides of houses and the bodies of spacecraft.

Metals are not the only materials that are products of human transformation of natural resources. From the earliest historical times people have manipulated fire and earth to make ceramics and glasses. In the nineteenth century, these materials, like so many others, moved from the realm of the craftsman's workroom into that of the factory, and in so doing they became more akin in both their working and their functions to the manufactured materials. Although a number of distinguished glass manufacturers flourished in America by the mid-nineteenth century, the new regime of industrialized glass was ushered in by a number of late-nineteenth-century entrepreneurs, such as Edward D. Libbey, John Ford, and the Houghtons of Corning, New York. Libbey was instrumental in making glass bottles the ubiquitous and cheap containers that they became in the nineteenth century. Ford and his Pittsburgh companions succeeded where others had failed in establishing plate-glass manufacture as a large-scale American industry. And, under the leadership of several generations of the Houghton family, the Corning Glass Works demonstrated how science and advanced techniques could produce a variety of glasses for almost every technical need, from chemical ware to light bulbs.

Rubber represented a different side of the nineteenth century's extension of material capabilities. South American Indians had been observed to use rubber as long ago as the voyages of Columbus, but Europeans were very slow to find applications for it. Indians used the sticky, elastic sap from "hevea" trees to waterproof footwear and clothing and to make flexible drinking vessels and bouncing balls. The raw material, however, was very temperamental, becoming gummy and smelly in hot weather, growing brittle and cracking in colder climates. It acquired the name "rubber" in the late eighteenth century

when small pieces began to be used as erasers to "rub out" pencil marks, but it was not until the 1820s that broader uses were developed. Charles Macintosh and Thomas Hancock in Britain pioneered mechanical and chemical treatments to make rubber more useful, but their products, ranging from rain gear to inflatable pillows, were still not fully satisfactory.

The challenge of making rubber stable at a wide range of temperatures and conditions preoccupied Charles Goodyear for nearly ten years before he discovered in 1839 how to use sulphur, white lead, and heat to make stable rubber products. His process, "vulcanization," allowed the manufacture of a variety of goods, from flexible rubber hoses and gloves to hard rubber for combs, battery jars, and flooring. The growth of the rubber industry in the United States was slow but steady through much of the nineteenth century, but at century's end new technologies emerged, first bicycles and then automobiles, that made rubber not just a useful material but a strategic commodity. The armies and airplanes of the twentieth century needed their tires, so rubber and its sources became matters of great political concern. The importance of natural rubber gave an extra push to efforts aimed at making synthetic rubber. In our own time rubber has moved from the realm of the manufactured materials to that of the synthetic.

Synthetic Materials

One of the most distinctive characteristics of the modern world is the prevalence of new materials—substances completely unknown to our ancestors. These are products of an age in which scientific knowledge combined with technology to promote the idea that there are no limits to the kinds of materials we can make for our own purposes. The plastics are the most spectacular example of synthetic materials, but new glasses and ceramics, complex new alloys and composites, semiconductors, and superconductors are likewise products of new abilities and new confidence in manipulating the building blocks of nature.

The story of the synthetics takes place mainly in the twentieth century, but, like so much else in modern science and technology, it has its beginnings in the middle of the last century. At just the time that industry was beginning to flourish with the expanding use of the metals and other manufactured materials, a few imaginative inventors were beginning to seek ways of getting around the limitations of what nature had to offer in the way of trees, minerals, and other traditional materials and putting together the most basic parts of matter into novel and useful combinations. In the mid-nineteenth century this effort was primarily the work of clever craftsmen. Many of them combined a thorough knowledge of existing materials and intelligent experimentation with a wide range of substances to produce important innovations, such as the first plastics and new alloys. In subsequent decades, however, the rapidly growing

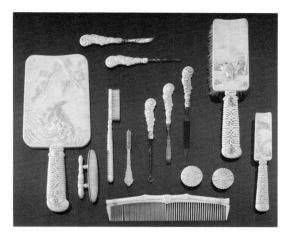

This celluloid toilet set, made to imitate carved ivory, is a particularly elaborate example of a popular early-twentieth-century middle-class possession.

science of chemistry came to play the leading role in directing inventors to new possibilities. In our own day the making of new materials has become almost commonplace, just one of the many sources of technological novelty that seems constantly to remake our world.

There can be no question that the ubiquitous synthetics make some things in life easier, cheaper, and more pleasing, perhaps most obviously in the home. The polyester clothing that keeps the ironing board folded in the corner, the Formica countertop that wipes clean with a damp cloth, the glass-ceramic dish that goes from freezer to oven, the lightweight toys strung over a baby's crib, the long-wearing wall-to-wall carpet—they all testify to the accepted role of new materials in twentieth-century life. But in the midst of all this there are questions to be pondered, about how well we human beings really adjust to a world more and more of our own making, about how well our earth

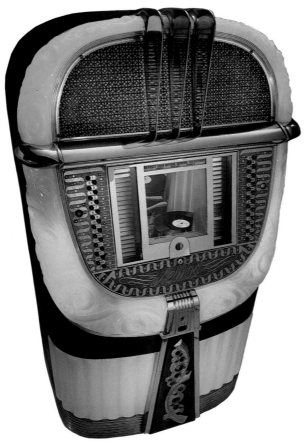

Plastics such as transparent acrylic and colorful acetate gave a whole new dimension to jukeboxes, such as this 1946 Model A from AMI.

can absorb the materials that it never knew, about what our striving for constant novelty and artifice says about our most basic values. These are not questions to be answered glibly, as uncomfortable as they may make us. They are, above all, not questions to be addressed without some appreciation of just what this synthetic world is all about and where it came from.

In the first half of the nineteenth cen-

tury the spirit of experiment and novelty drove inventors and would-be inventors to seek both fortunes and reputations in every realm of technology. New machines, from locomotives to sewing machines, were the most spectacular fruits of this march of progress, but gadgets, tools, and little improvements to all areas of life and work were part of the swelling flood of ideas and dreams that poured into the Patent Office. New materials were not a major part of all this, for the capabilities of chemistry were still meager compared with those of mechanics. By mid-century, however, some imaginative experimenters had begun to make efforts to create materials just as others invented and built machines. In some cases inventors had clear ideas about how to use such new materials. But just as often would-be inventors were driven simply by their belief that a new material was possible, and sustained by their faith that a good material would find suitable uses that might, in turn, make its creator rich.

Among the first artificial plastics were celluloid, invented in 1869, and Bakelite, created in 1907. (A detailed discussion of these two crucial plastics begins the next section, "New Materials, New Choices.") By the 1920s the introduction and use of plastics like Bakelite, celluloid, and others had begun to change the appearance and "feel" of life. The ease with which the plastics could be produced and shaped made them particularly appealing to the new professional industrial designers who were beginning to have an important influence on the styles and products of American manufacturers. Streamlining— the widespread use of shapes originally designed to reduce wind resistance and increase speed affected the form of everything from windows to lamps to radio cabinets. The new plastics were obvious materials for a style that emphasized flow and smoothness.

As the century wore on, growing understanding of chemical processes and possibilities yielded a flood of new plastics. Much of this progress was linked to the emergence of a new field of chemistry devoted to polymers and other giant molecules. In the 1930s chemical theory combined with the ambitions of giant companies, both in Europe and the United States, to push ahead the development of a whole host of "polys": polyethylene, polystyrene, polytetrafluoroethylene (PTFE or Teflon), polymethyl methacrylate (acrylics, such as Plexiglas or Lucite), polyvinyl chloride (PVC or simply "vinyl"), the polyesters, and polyisoprene (artificial rubber). Closely related were the new artificial fibers, such as rayon and other cellulose-based materials, and the polyamides, most notably nylon, one of the most spectacular products of fundamental chemical research in indus-

try. By the beginning of the Second World War, chemists had managed to change the substance of the world, and much else with it. University and corporate laboratories now overshadowed the rubber trees of Malaya and the silkworms of China as strategic and vital resources.

Plastics were perhaps the most novel elements in this new material world of the mid-twentieth century, but they were not the only ones. The needs of exotic new technologies such as aviation and electronics fostered the creation of advanced new alloys, forms of aluminum, steel, and other metals with combinations of properties hardly imaginable to earlier generations. Ceramics became not simply important mass-produced materials, but sophisticated products of the laboratories of the chemist and the materials engineer. They were capable of withstanding the heat and stress of a space capsule's reentry into the earth's atmosphere, returning from a voyage to the moon.

Glassmakers transformed the image of an ancient material by flaunting a hitherto unsuspected versatility. The effort to im-

Amplifier section of a high-powered laser, using discs of glass doped with the rare element neodymium as the lasing material.

35

prove the performance of railway signal lanterns yielded Pyrex, which provided everyone from chemist to cook with tougher, more reliable glassware. Pulling glass out into long fibers produced fiberglass, a material used for fireproof draperies, surfboards, and a motley host of other products. Even more sophisticated glass fibers became the basis for fiber optics, a revolution in communications still in the making. And by making the tiniest of variations in the composition of their product, some glassmakers produced a kind of glass that, with the right energy, could yield the incredible light of the laser. In other realms of electronics the same silicon that is common to almost all glass came to serve a very different role, providing the material foundations for the microelectronics revolution. The "chip" that is the soul of the computer and much else in modern technology depends on the behavior of the semiconductor material on which it is built, crystals of silicon, germanium, or more exotic substances.

Our late twentieth-century world looks very different from that of our ancestors. A world of more people and more things

is necessarily a world of less nature. At the most obvious level birds, trees, and fields give way to airplanes, highways, and shopping centers. Perhaps a bit less evident, but no less true, is that a world of more science is also a world less natural than before. Not only do the mysteries of nature and its wonderful processes and constructions become a bit less awe-inspiring in the glare of science's penetrating light, but it is our wont—perhaps our fate—to change things even as we come to understand them. Nowhere is this more true than in the shaping and reshaping of our manmade environment. Just as we come to know what makes a tree tall and strong, we seek to do better than its wood for our own purposes. As we find out the constitution of the fibers, the clays, and the metals upon which we have long depended, we not only transform them but we replace them in our artifacts. In replacing them we have constructed a world much more of our own design. As such, it is a world that may or may not be more to our liking, but it is certainly a world for which we bear more responsibility, for good or ill.

This Electrolux vacuum cleaner of the late 1930s illustrates how industrial designers used such novel materials as chromed steel and plastics to create distinctive designs, even in utilitarian objects.

New Materials, New Choices

In the last century and a half there has taken place a revolution in materials just as profound and important as the mechanical and electrical revolutions that gave us entirely new ways of using and thinking about energy. The materials revolution, like its predecessors, has changed not only the technologies themselves but the role of these technologies in our civilization. We see materials and their possibilities in very different ways than did our ancestors. We think differently about what is possible and what is not, about how materials and objects should behave and function, about the beauty, the fitness, even the wisdom of the objects that we make and use. New materials mean new choices, and the choices we make tell us a great deal about our culture and ourselves.

The materials revolution was caused in part by the growth of scientific knowledge in the nineteenth century, especially knowledge of chemistry. By mid-century scientists had useful theories to explain how chemicals combined to make compounds, new techniques for making a wide variety of substances novel and familiar, and a rapidly expanding sense of the practical and commercial importance of their work. The new power of chemistry is only part of the story, however, for the revolutionary potential of chemical knowledge was realized only because of new attitudes toward the material world. For centuries people had assumed that the materials that nature provided for human use were limited in their form and function. Although artisans and inventors

might make new contrivances for harnessing power sources or for transporting goods and people, traditional materials seemed to most people to define the limits of what was available. The spirit of invention and enterprise that was so characteristic of the nineteenth century, however, led to another way of looking at things. People began to seek out new materials just as they had sought fortune and success with other inventions. Slowly such efforts yielded important products, the foundations of individual and corporate wealth. By our own century the search for new materials had become an accepted, even indispensable part of the economic and technological world.

In spite of the spirit of innovation that drove the search for new materials, success required more than simple knowledge and technical skill. The discovery of a new material frequently posed a special problem for the entrepreneur, for the best uses or markets for a novel substance were rarely obvious. The properties of a new material have to be found out, sometimes with great effort, and its uses must be discovered through experiment and trial. Typically the would-be inventor was driven by ideas about the possible uses of a new material, but these notions were time and again found to be chimerical. The inventor of the first plastic, celluloid, was seeking a good material for billiard balls, but his wonderful new substance failed at the task. The promoters of aluminum speculated about all sorts of uses for their metal, only to find that the world was not ready for it. Bakelite, the first completely synthetic polymer, was discovered in pursuit of a substitute for shellac—a use that gave only a hint of its true potential. In the twentieth century, as new materials have come to be the fruit of systematic, corporate research, the development of uses and markets has also become more systematic. And advanced technical knowledge makes possible the creation of some new materials to order—with properties correctly predicted by theory and created to fill to specific needs.

Even if an inventor understands a material's properties and uses at the outset, all new materials still present new choices and new opportunities—with unpredictable consequences. The first plastics, for example, were used to expand the universe of affordable luxury for the growing middle classes of the nineteenth century. These materials could be colored and shaped in wonderful ways, even imitating the appearance of precious substances like ivory or pearl. Made into combs, brushes, and dozens of other pieces of personal equipment, plastics like celluloid provided handsome alternatives to plainer substances like rubber or cheap metal. Be-

The racist claim that celluloid collars and cuffs would eliminate the need for oriental laundrymen was used on a number of late-nineteenth-century advertising cards.
Courtesy of the Collection of Business Americana, Archives Center, National Museum of American History

A PAGEANT OF EN[...]

Every piece . . . every size and shape . . . is especially design[...] to meet a specific problem. Of greater importance is the f[...] that each piece represents the specialized engineering, desi[...] ing and molding skill that make these products possible. Th[...] represent the care and attention to detail that is accorded eve[...]

Injection molders of Tenite; Lucite; Lumarith; Plastacele; Crystallite; Vinylite; Polystyrene and other Thermoplastic Materials

Custom Injection Molding Exclusively

Plastics manufacturers and fabricators advertised their material as the stuff of a colorful cornucopia.

cause many of the later plastics could be easily and rapidly molded into shapes with flowing lines, they contributed to the rise of new concepts of design and styling in an enormous variety of objects, ranging from chairs to radios to pencil sharpeners. The development of inexpensive plastics for packaging, replacing biodegradable paper products or easily recyclable metal ones, imposes complex economic and envi-

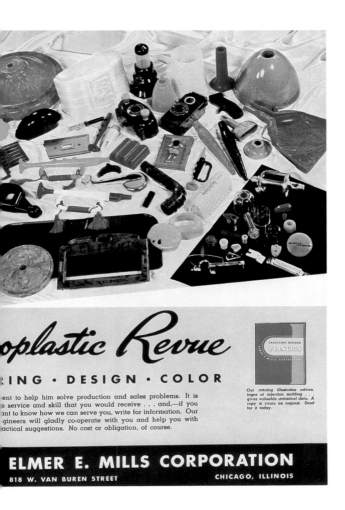

Plastics Pioneers

The most striking of all new materials—
the ones that proclaim their novelty most
boldly and unambiguously—are plastics.
The twentieth century looks and feels different from any earlier time due largely to
these materials. At the same time that
plastics are heralds and symbols of our
modernity, they are also the source of
some ambiguous feelings. Just as some
people admire plastics for their versatility
and utility, others sometimes scorn them
as cheap, imitative, or lesser substitutes
for valued natural materials. Just like the
materials themselves, these perceptions
color our world; they affect the way we
feel about our things, our sense of the
lasting value of our creations, and how we
regard the relationship between the artificial world and the natural one. This pecu-
liar role of plastics in our culture is associated in some ways with the special
properties of these materials, but it is due
even more to their history.

The materials that we today call plastics
are all "polymers," that is, they are made
up of giant molecules consisting of
hundreds or thousands of atoms. Other
materials, such as metals or ceramics, consist of much smaller molecular structures,
often held together in some arrangement
of crystals. Organic materials, from straw
to wood to leather to bone, are polymers,
most commonly made of either cellulose
or protein. These polymers, like the man-
made ones, consist generally of carbon,
along with varying amounts of oxygen,
hydrogen, nitrogen (in proteins), and occasionally a small amount of other elements,
like sulphur or phosphorous. Even though

ronmental choices on a society reluctant to
face them. The use of aluminum, stainless
steel, and chrome in building fostered new
ideas in architecture and interior design,
providing the basis for a "machine age"
look in the 1920s and 1930s. Even more
exotic metals made possible such extraordinary new technologies as jet aircraft and
nuclear reactors. The common thread
through all these examples is the capacity
of novel substances to give individuals and
societies new choices where few or none
had existed before.

nineteenth-century scientists did not think in terms of giant molecules, they were beginning to understand which elements composed living things and to manipulate these elements in some of the same ways that nature did. This ability spawned astonishing new products, of which the plastics were at first rather humble examples.

Much more spectacular to the eyes of mid-nineteenth-century men and women were the coal-tar dyes. Building on a generation of pathbreaking laboratory work by German and French chemists, the artificial dye industry began with the work of a young English student, William Henry Perkin. At college in London in 1856, Perkin was given by his German professor an "impossible" laboratory assignment, the synthesis of quinine from the relatively simple waste products of coal tar. In the course of this work he produced a deep purple product, whose colors so intrigued him that he sent a sample to a dyer. In barely a year Perkin's "mauve" had caused a sensation, and the search for other artificial dyes was on. In short order chemists produced a host of new colors, including magenta, fuchsia, and synthetic versions of indigo blue and Congo red. Almost overnight synthetic dyes wiped out the ancient industries that produced vegetable dyes and introduced the world to modern chemistry's potential for creating a new order of things.

On the heels of the dyes came other products, some of them even more valuable. Chemists soon learned to make from coal-tar derivatives and other sources substances such as vanillin (artificial vanilla), tupineol (artificial lilac), ionone (artificial violet), and other synthetic perfumes and flavorings. Valuable drugs also came from the laboratory, such as salicylic acid, better known as aspirin. As wonderful as these and many similar products were, they were not polymers. The dyes, flavorings, and drugs were all compounds with much smaller molecules.

The first plastics were not artificial polymers, but instead came from one of nature's most common polymers, cellulose. In the 1840s the Swiss chemist Christian Schönbein discovered how to react ordinary pure cellulose (as, for instance, cotton) with nitric and sulphuric acid to produce "pyroxylin." This substance looked much like the cotton it came from, but it behaved differently. For one thing, it burned quite violently. In fact, one form of it came to be known as guncotton—an important new explosive. Pyroxylin was also soluble in common solvents, like alcohol and ether. The syrupy solution was called collodion and its tendency to form a thin, clear film as it dried led to its rapid adoption as a kind of liquid bandage. In the 1850s collodion became the basis for important new photographic processes. A few dabblers—not really chemists but rather materials craftsmen—began trying to see if they could use the same substance that produced the thin film to make a more substantial material, a plastic. Celluloid was the result of their work.

Celluloid was invented in 1869 by an Albany, New York, printer and mechanic, John Wesley Hyatt. Hyatt had been dabbling for years with useful molding compositions when he decided to try his hand at making an imitation of ivory. One inspiration for this was the announcement by a New York City billiards supply house of a large reward for a practical replacement for the ivory used in billiard balls. After considerable experimentation Hyatt finally combined pyroxylin with the aromatic gum camphor. When he mixed correct proportions of these substances under heat and pressure, the result was a hard, uniform material. Celluloid displayed from the outset the versatility of forming and working that is one of the most distinctive characteristics of the plastics. It could be cut, polished, molded, colored, carved, and shaped in a variety of ways. It resisted water, oils, and many acids. Since pyroxylin was made of cotton or some other cellulose-based material that had been "nitrated," the new material was dubbed celluloid by Hyatt, and it is referred to as a "nitrocellulose" plastic.

In 1870 John Wesley Hyatt and his brother Isaiah established the first company for making and selling celluloid products. The Albany Dental Plate Company, however, was a failure. Although their new material was in many ways far superior to the hard rubber then often used for dental plates, it also had some drawbacks. Perhaps the most serious was celluloid's tendency to lose its shape at the temperature of very hot water or food, and apparently numerous reports of embarrassing episodes with dentures made their way back to Albany. After less than a year the Hyatts expanded their efforts beyond the unfortunate dental plates and organized the Celluloid Manufacturing Company. The lessons of their first marketing experiences were not forgotten. Every plastics maker subsequently had also to learn that success in the real world of consumers and business required the most careful matching of material to product, supplemented by much work at education and persuasion.

In the 1870s and 1880s the celluloid makers steadily found marketable uses for their material. Celluloid was especially suited for fancy effects, such as imitating tortoiseshell and mother-of-pearl. It began appearing most prominently in combs, brushes, mirrors, and other small personal items. The most popular form for such goods was imitation ivory. Manufacturers discovered clever methods not only to color celluloid the proper tones of yellow-white but also to give it the same slightly irregular striations of genuine ivory. Other ingenious techniques arose for giving pure white celluloid the look and texture of fine linen, and celluloid collars and cuffs became well-known products. These efforts and others created modest though reliable markets for celluloid, but they also branded it as largely an imitative material rather than a substance to be valued for its own appearance and properties. Celluloid's image as a "cheap imitation" of finer natural substances was an important, if often unfortunate, legacy to later plastics.

In at least one area, however, celluloid demonstrated how important plastics could be in creating new technical possibilities. In the mid-1880s George Eastman set out to create and market a new system of photography, one that would transform it from a complex craft into a popular and readily accessible pastime. But a major stumbling block was the lack of a suitable material for the roll film that he wanted to put into his cheap cameras. After several years of trying alternatives, Eastman and his young chemist, Henry Reichenbach, discovered how to adapt celluloid to the purpose. The first celluloid film for Eastman's cameras went on sale in August

Boontonware, made from melamine formaldehyde resin, was a popular variety of unbreakable dishes in the years after World War II.

1889, and its enthusiastic reception guaranteed the success of the Kodak camera. Within only a few years a number of experimenters in motion pictures tried the film for their new medium. Later references to movie stars and theaters as "celluloid personalities" and "celluloid palaces," testify to the contribution of the plastic to cinematography.

Other cellulose plastics followed, the best known of these being cellulose acetate; unlike celluloid, it was not flammable, and it could be made crystal clear. The adoption of acetate for "safety film" in the 1920s and 1930s was an important step in making motion picture theaters safer. Also appearing in the 1920s was cellophane, a cellulose-based plastic that helped to revolutionize the packaging and sale of food.

Whatever its popular or technical contributions might be, celluloid was still a limited material with a modest place in the scheme of things by the end of the nineteenth century. The real contribution of plastics to modern life was the result of the creation of even more novel substances in the twentieth century, substances that would spring from the same kind of advanced and creative chemistry that the synthetic dyes and drugs had depended on. The herald of this new age was Bakelite, the first synthetic polymer plastic.

Unlike celluloid, Bakelite was the invention of an accomplished, well-trained chemist. Leo Hendrik Baekeland was born in Belgium and received there an advanced education in chemistry, becoming a professor at the University of Ghent in 1887. Soon afterwards, however, he visited the United States and stayed in the hope of winning fame and fortune by applying his specialized knowledge to practical problems. His first success was a much-improved photographic paper, and his sale of this invention to George Eastman in 1899 made Baekeland a rich man at age thirty-six. He then proceeded to dabble in his backyard laboratory on a variety of chemical problems. He came up with little of interest until he turned his attention to reactions between two fairly simple organic compounds, phenol and formaldehyde. Many chemists knew that these two substances would react, producing a hard, insoluble material that was difficult to analyze. But Baekeland studied the reaction with great care, varying amounts and conditions to see if he could control it. He reasoned that if he could come up with a way to apply a coating of this tough substance to other materials, like wood, he might have a substitute for

Washing machine impeller molded of Bakelite phenolic resin

shellac or other varnishes. Instead, he came up with much more.

In a series of experiments in mid-1907, Baekeland learned how to manipulate the phenol-formaldehyde reaction to produce a varnish and a solid, moldable resin. He quickly recognized the possible importance of this discovery, dubbed the new material Bakelite, and after several more months of work, announced to the world his discovery:

> It makes excellent billiard balls of which [the] elasticity is very close to that of ivory, in short, it can be used for similar purposes like knobs, buttons, knife handles, for which plastics are generally used. But its use for such fancy articles has not much appealed to my efforts as long as there are so many more important applications for engineering purposes.

Baekeland's assessment of the importance of Bakelite was remarkably on target. Combined with any of several possible fillers, the new resin made a durable, easily formed material that was excellent for many workaday applications. Bakelite's resistance to heat, electricity, and chemical action made it the perfect substance for insulating and protecting a host of products, from telephones to cookware. Ordinarily the material would not burn in a fire, but only char. Its versatility as a binder for materials like sawdust, fabric, or paper made it possible to vary the density, texture, and brittleness of finished products to a wide range of specifications. Fillers often made it dark and opaque, so Bakelite was not usually made with the fancy imitative effects so common to celluloid. But even in the realm of jewelry the durability and moldability of the resin made it popular for bracelets and beads. Phenolic resins also appeared in colorful radio cabinets, often under the trade name Catalin. When joined with wood, paper, or cloth, artificial resins became the basis for important laminated materials, such as Formica, Micarta, and plywood.

Finding marketable uses for Bakelite was easier than for earlier plastics largely because of its versatility and technical potential. But another contributing factor was simply that, by the early twentieth century, manufacturers and consumers had a good idea of how to use plastics.

The introduction of Bakelite spurred on chemists' investigations of other possibilities for synthetic materials. The 1920s and 1930s saw a flowering of plastics, for now large corporations put their faith and money into the effort. Just a few examples will give a hint of the outpouring of this

Nylon stockings created a sensation
when they first appeared in 1939.

Courtesy of the Hagley Museum and Library

period. In 1926 a chemist for rubber manufacturer B.F. Goodrich discovered how
to make adhesives and sheets from polyvinyl chloride, and "vinyl" became one of
the most common plastics. In 1930 the
giant German firm of I.G. Farben put
polystyrene on the market, providing a
material of extraordinary versatility. Another German company, Röhm and Haas,
brought out Plexiglas (polymethyl methacrylate) in 1935, and the technical and aesthetic possibilities of a crystal-clear plastic
were soon exploited widely.

The most spectacular triumph of industrial chemical research in the 1930s was
nylon. Introduced to the public in 1938,
nylon was the culmination of almost ten
years of research at the Du Pont Company under the direction of Wallace H.
Carothers. When he came to Du Pont in
1928, Carothers was a thirty-two-year-old
with a Ph.D. in chemistry from the University of Illinois. He had taught both
there and at Harvard University. Du Pont
lured him to their laboratories with the
promise of the best facilities, access to
bright young graduate chemists, and a
broadly defined mission devoted to fundamental research. In his work Carothers
sought a better understanding of the reactions that produced polymers and how to
apply these reactions to different chemicals. An early product of these investigations was polychlorobutadiene, a synthetic
rubber marketed by Du Pont under the
name neoprene.

At the same time that Carothers's research was getting under way, industry
was turning more of its attention to the
production of artificial fibers. The first
such fiber had been made in France in the
1880s from pyroxylin, the same chemical

44

used to make celluloid. By the 1920s another artificial fiber with a cellulose base, rayon, had become an important commercial product. Carothers, his associate, Julian Hill, and their research team sought to make a fiber not from natural polymers like cellulose but from the synthesis of simple organic compounds. They discovered that some artificial polymers could be pulled out into threadlike strands that when stretched became strong and flexible. Finding just which polymer would give the best results from such treatment took more work, but by 1935 the Du Pont researchers had synthesized a group of polymers with much the same chemistry as silk—the polyamides. In mid-1937 yarn spun from a polyamide was knit into experimental stockings, and the following year nylon went into production.

Unfortunately, Carothers did not live to see nylon's success. But few materials have experienced such an immediate technical and commercial triumph. When the first nylon stockings went on sale in 1939,

Wallace H. Carothers
Courtesy of the Hagley Museum and Library

they caused an instant sensation, promising liberation from the tight supplies and fickle behavior of natural silk. Other nylon fabrics and fibers soon followed, although in early 1942 the U.S. government laid claim to all nylon for the war effort, most notably for parachutes, but also for flak vests, tire cords, and rope. The strategic significance of having a durable and versatile silk substitute at just the point that Asian supplies were cut off by war was a widely appreciated lesson. After the war nylon's toughness, elasticity, and chemical and electrical resistance made it popular for molded items, from combs to machine gears to insulators. Perhaps even more significantly for the future, nylon brought home the potential of modern chemistry to create materials that could rapidly change any realm of modern life, from fashion to war.

The same year that Du Pont began manufacturing nylon, another Du Pont chemist, Roy Plunkett, discovered a very different material, polytetrafluoroethylene (PTFE). An accidental product of experiments with a class of materials known as "fluorocarbons," PTFE had extraordinary properties. It resisted heat, electricity, corrosion, and a wide range of chemical and biochemical activities and possessed the lowest friction of any solid material. It took Du Pont ten years to bring PTFE, which they dubbed Teflon, to market, and it took yet another decade for Teflon to find widespread uses, which range today from cookware to artificial arteries. Teflon's twenty-year odyssey from laboratory to kitchen, operating room, and electrical shop typified the experiences of other materials in new generation of polymers: The properties of the material were

Lily Chair, designed by Erwine and Estelle Laverne
in 1959, made entirely of acrylic except for the
cushion.

radically different from anything else; it
could not simply be a cheaper or moder-
ately improved substitute for a traditional
substance; and its uses had to be discovered and then communicated to the rest of
the world.

Teflon's story shares some elements
with many other stories in the history of
materials. But the new polymers (and
many other developments in ceramics,
glasses, alloys, and "biomaterials") frequently seem to present questions so new
that even an age jaded by constant change
and innovation has to struggle to cope
with them. New forms have joined new
compositions to extend the reach of the

polymers. We are often only vaguely
aware of these, but just a moment's reflec-
tion and a few examples will suggest their
pervasiveness.

The first foamed plastics were introduced in the late 1920s. Both soft foam
plastics such as foam rubber and rigid
forms such as polyurethane began to appear commercially in the next decade.
Now, everything from egg cartons to insulation to seat cushions are are made
from these airy plastics.

Nylon did not long remain the only
completely synthetic fiber, though not until the 1950s did the full impact of other
fibers come to be felt. Du Pont's Orlon
acrylic went into large-scale production in
1950, and in a couple of years the first
Orlon-cotton blend came to market. Only
a few months later, in early 1953, Brooks
Brothers introduced its first Dacron-cotton
shirt, and the "wash and wear" revolution
had begun. Dacron was Du Pont's trade-
mark for its fiber made from polyethylene
terephthalate (PET). This material, known
generically as a polyester, turned out to be
extraordinarily versatile. Films made from
PET began in the mid-1950s to be used
for photography, recording tape, and food
packaging.

Reinforcing plastics with various substances has been important since the introduction of Bakelite early in the century,
but the properties and forms of composite
materials have expanded enormously since
then. Born as a phenolic resin and paper
laminate for electrical insulation, Formica
began to be used in the 1920s for decorative surfaces. In the next decade Formica
appeared in everything from table tops to
entire walls. The mid-1930s saw the introduction of fiberglass integrated into a

number of synthetic resins, the most important of which turned out to be polyesters. After World War II epoxy resins began to be used where high strength was required, and fiber-reinforced plastics made their way into everything from pleasure boats to subway seats to radar installations. The development of new fibers such as carbon and Kevlar (a polyamide) have enabled an even greater variety of properties to be conjured up as the needs arise.

And the needs *will* arise, not just for a new resin here or new kind of film there, but for whatever new thing the commercial and technical mind can imagine. Some of them will be trivial or even silly, others will be lifesaving or thought-provoking or simply helpful for some small task of daily living. But the key lesson of the plastics—and, indeed, of all the novel materials of our time—is that new materials do mean new opportunities and new choices, bounded on the one side only by imagination and on the other by responsibility.

Mid-nineteenth-century railroad lantern of tin and glass

Metals of Magic :
Steel and Aluminum

A century ago it was new metals, rather than plastics or any other substances, that would have struck the ordinary observer as the materials of modernity. The key technologies and products of the late nineteenth century were overwhelmingly based on metal, primarily iron and steel. When the traditional metals, such as wrought iron and the copper alloys, began slowly to give way to others, such as steel and aluminum, the change was widely perceived as an important one, with obscure social and economic implications. Just as with other new materials, the new metals offered society new choices, which elicited both hope and uncertainty.

In both quantity and impact the most important new metal of the nineteenth century was not really new at all. Skilled craftsmen had made steel for three thousand years before radical changes in the processes of manufacture gave it an entirely new place in technical and economic life. Sword blades of steel were particularly prized, for they took advantage of the metal's wonderful combination of hardness, resilience, and strength. The modern metallurgist recognizes the superior properties of steel as the result of a delicate balance between its two components, iron and carbon. For most of the metal's history, however, it was not even suspected that steel was an alloy. This most prized product of the forge was generally thought to be an exceptionally pure form of iron produced by rigorous cleansing and purfiying. By the beginning of the

nineteenth century chemists recognized that the primary distinction between steel and other ferrous metals was that steel contained a measurable amount of carbon but not more than about 2 percent. With more carbon, the material became cast iron, easily melted and molded, but quite brittle; with little or no carbon, the metal became workable ("ductile," the metallurgist would say) but impossible to cast. Despite this knowledge, making steel cheaply and in quantity remained an elusive goal until mid-century.

The new processes for making steel introduced by Henry Bessemer, William Kelly, and others allowed steel to displace other forms of iron in the last decades of the nineteenth century. At the same time, other experimenters were able to make new kinds of steel with previously unimagined properties. In 1868 the Englishman Robert Mushet discovered that adding 5 to 8 percent tungsten to molten Bessemer steel and allowing it to cool slowly produced a material that retained (or increased) its hardness even when red hot. This was the first of the tool steels, so-called for their value in cutting other metals. At about the same time, it was discovered that chromium had a similar effect on steel, and eventually a chromium-tungsten alloy emerged as the most common tool steel. In 1898 the Americans Frederick Winslow Taylor and Maunsel White discovered that cooling the steel more quickly allowed tools to cut even faster and to get even hotter. Their product became known as "high-speed" steel.

Many other steel alloys emerged in the late nineteenth and early twentieth centuries. The use of nickel steel for armorplating warships contributed to the naval

Drawing Press, No. 1½.

(Scale ¾ of an inch to the foot.)

Clutch Patented December 27th, 1870.

This drawing press was constructed about 1882 by the firm of E. W. Bliss in Brooklyn, New York, and operated for almost a century to press shapes out of sheet steel.

48

arms race between the European powers before World War I. Adding manganese to steel increases its hardness considerably, thus allowing the construction of the giant mining machinery that began ripping away at mountains in the American West and other parts of the world at the turn of the century. Relatively high amounts of chromium (up to 18 percent or more) can be added to steel to enhance various properties. The giant arch bridge that James Eads put across the Mississippi River at St. Louis in 1874 used chromium steel. In the years just before World War I there emerged the most spectacular alloy of them all, stainless steel, made with large amounts of chromium and lesser quantities of nickel (and sometimes other metals as well). The creation of a steel that was impervious to rust and corrosion became a boon to everyone from surgeons and architects to diners and shavers.

Even more novel than the new steels were the entirely new metals that appeared in the late nineteenth century. The most important of these was aluminum, and in its story we can see the wonder with which men and women of the last century greeted the creations of modern science. Here was a metal unknown until the 1840s, although its ore was believed to be the most common of all metallic ores in the earth's crust. Admired for its silvery color and its resistance to tarnish or corrosion, aluminum was most remarkable for its light weight—aluminum has a density a quarter that of silver and one-third that of iron or steel. Journalists of the 1850s wrote in glowing terms of the "silver from clay," and of the possible revolution in industry and daily life that might ensue once cheap aluminum became available.

In the mid-1850s the French chemist Henri St. Claire Deville devised a process to move aluminum from the laboratory into the factory, but the metal was still precious. For three decades it remained rare, used for fine and expensive items such as opera glasses, ladies' fans, and the tableware of Napolean III. The amount of aluminum made in America was measured not in tons or pounds but in ounces. When in 1884 a one-hundred-ounce pyramid of aluminum was used for the apex of the Washington Monument, the metal was chosen not only for its great conductivity (it served as a kind of lightning rod) and its color, but also because its high price made it an appropriate finishing touch to the great structure.

The great cost of aluminum was not due to the price of its ore, for the oxide of aluminum ("alumina") was a common, easily prepared material. The problem came from the high cost of metallic sodium, one of the few materials that would react with the alumina to yield the pure metal. The search for an alternative process was a popular goal of inventors in the 1870s and 1880s, both in Europe and in America. In 1886 the elusive alternative was found, not by seasoned chemists or experienced metal workers, but by two young amateurs, working independently in modest home-laboratories. The processes invented by Paul L.T. Héroult in France and Charles Martin Hall in the United States depended on electrical, not chemical, extraction of the metal. They relied on efficient and reliable electrical generators, which had been available for only a few years, and on a method found in the late 1880s of making very pure alumina. They succeeded where others had failed, however, primarily because they discovered how to use the aluminum salt, cryolite, to dissolve the alumina in their electrical reduction pots. An electric current separated metallic aluminum out of a solution of molten cryolite and alumina, and the cost of the process depended almost solely on the price of alumina (which was fairly cheap) and electricity. To take advantage of the cheap electricity, the first giant aluminum plants were thus built near hydroelectric installations.

Only a couple of years after Hall set up the Pittsburgh Reduction Company (later Alcoa) in 1888, the price of the metal had dropped from about twelve dollars a

SEE PAGE 52

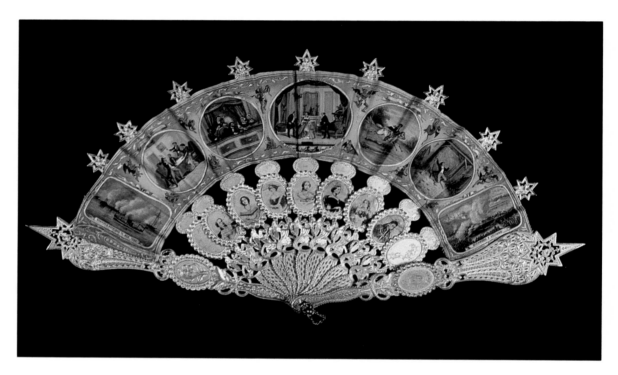

This aluminum fan was made for display at the Paris Exposition of 1867, when aluminum was still a rare and precious material. It is decorated with pictures of the queens of Europe as well as scenes of the assassination of Abraham Lincoln and the pursuit of the assassins.

A Materials Showcase

The *Swamp Rat XXX* is a top fuel drag-ster—one of the most astonishing racing cars in the world. As such, it has no purpose except to carry its driver safely as it accelerates as fast as possible. The *Swamp Rat XXX* is an example of how modern materials and design combine to accomplish things never done before. Designed and built by Don Garlits, it was the first dragster to exceed a speed of 270 miles per hour, a feat accomplished in its maiden race. The low, sleek profile of the car was critical to its performance, but a key contributor to that profile and to the *Swamp Rat*'s rapid acceleration, was the extraordinarily complex combination of materials throughout the vehicle.

The nosepiece and the airfoil are made of a composite of fibers made from the polyamide Kevlar and carbon. The cockpit canopy is made from the polycarbonate Lexan. The chassis uses a chromium-molybdenum alloy steel; other metals include stainless steel, nickel steel, silicon steel, bronze, tin, copper, brass, aluminum, lead, silver, gold, magnesium, titanium, and indium.

Advanced materials used for safety include Kevlar in the blankets designed to contain pieces thrown off by a break-up; another polyamide, Nomex, valued for its fire-resistance, for the parachute packs and lines; and a third polyamide, nylon, for the parachute itself. Other polymers are used throughout, including fluorocarbons (such as Teflon), neoprene, Bakelite, and silicones (polymers based on silicon rather than carbon).

51

pound to two, and prices continued to fall. This did not usher in, as some had prophesied, an "age of aluminum," however. Indeed, Charles Hall remarked with some dismay on the bars of unsold metal that piled up in his Pittsburgh plant. Making widespread and effective use of the new metal, in fact, required almost a half-century of constant experimenting and marketing, for aluminum was never cheaper than steel, had different properties from copper and its alloys, and quickly lost the glamor of "silver from clay."

The primary consumer of Hall's aluminum was the Pittsburgh steel industry, which discovered that a few ounces of aluminum added to molten steel reduced the air dissolved in the molten mixture. Getting manufacturers to use aluminum for their products was a much harder sell. When Hall sent a sample teakettle to a cookware maker to show how fine aluminum was for such a product, the manufacturer agreed and asked the people in Pittsburgh to send him several more cases to sell, but he protested that he couldn't possibly fabricate the strange new metal himself. Aluminum's light weight appealed to armies, which began to experiment with mess kits and other items to lighten the foot soldier's load. The sonorousness of pure aluminum attracted the attention of musical-instrument makers, although most soon discovered that the pure metal was too soft and that alloys had a poorer sound. Artificial limbs, fancy combs or pen sets, tableware, bicycle trim, machinists' patterns, and bathtubs were just some of the products tried out in aluminum's first decades. Some met with success, others were ignominious failures.

In the twentieth century aluminum has become one of the accepted materials of the craftsman as well as of everyday life, as shown in this 1940s pitcher from the Wendell August Forge.

Aluminum was fated to remain a rather minor metal in the scheme of things, except for the role it was to play in two of the twentieth century's most important technologies. By weight, aluminum is almost twice as conductive as copper, and as long-distance electric power transmission became increasingly important in the first decades of the new century, the virtues of aluminum transmission wire and cable, reinforced with steel for strength, made it a key material for the industry.

At the same time, the rise of aviation created a critical need for a material combining strength and light weight. Aluminum was used in minor ways in the very first airplanes, but it was the development of sophisticated aluminum alloys, especially Duralumin (slightly more than 3 percent copper and 1 percent magnesium and manganese), that enabled aluminum to displace other materials for aircraft frames in the 1920s, and so become a truly strategic material. U.S. aluminum production capacity tripled with the massive need for aircraft during the Second World War, and this new capacity became the foundation for a vastly expanded consumer market for the metal at war's end.

When, in the mid-1930s, the American historian and critic Lewis Mumford sought to describe what made the technol-

The large bulky radio set of the 1920s gave way in the 1930s to small table models. Colorful plastics, especially cast phenolic resins (such as Bakelite and Catalin), made the radio a vehicle for fashionable designs as well as a splash of bright color in American homes.

ogies of the twentieth century so different in feel, appearance, and social impact from those of the Industrial Revolution, he chose aluminum and plastics as the key materials of the new age. A central task of modern times, wrote Mumford, was the transformation of the machines and designs of iron so characteristic of industrial technology into more compact, lighter devices made of aluminum, advanced alloys, or artificial materials. Today we can see around us the results of this work. No longer are the creators of technology obsessed with bigness and strength; miniaturization, light weight, and quickness are primary values. New materials have been indispensable to this change. And they will continue to create and shape the changes of the future.

U.S. Capitol electrical station
Courtesy of the Architect of the Capitol

Material Messages

What is it made of? We can hardly ask a more ordinary question about a thing. We may seek a simple answer, giving us some idea of the value of an object or its purpose, or we might probe deeper in search of a more technical understanding of how something is put together or just where it came from. In most cases we know—or think we know—what things are made of. A person sitting in a chair made of wood is unlikely to ask just what kind of wood; no doubt few people holding a ballpoint pen wonder exactly what plastic it is made of. But confronted with an unusual sight—a transparent chair or a pen gleaming bright gold—people are more likely to probe further. Is it glass or is it plastic? Is it really gold or is it gilt or is it simply paint or some other bit of fakery? People want to know these things because the way in which they look at any object is shaped by their perceptions of what it is made of, and not knowing might leave them feeling vaguely confused or disturbed.

The materials of which a thing is made tell us something—usually without our being aware of it—about the thing, its makers, its users, its place in the scheme of things, whether it is ordinary or special. We are generally so accustomed to these "material messages" that we give them little or no thought, but in fact we constantly draw all sorts of conclusions about the values, purposes, status, sources, or worth of an object simply from its material make-up.

Flutes

The flute is one of the most ancient of musical instruments, though its modern form is one of the most technically sophisticated instrument designs. In its long history the flute has been made of almost every imaginable material, from the most precious, such as gold or ivory, to the very unassuming, such as wood or hard rubber. Because it can be easily turned and drilled, wood has a long and distinguished tradition in flutes, and its mellow tone still gives it a place. At various times in the past musicians and instrument makers have favored different woods. In the eighteenth century, for example, fruit woods such as pear and cherry were popular, along with boxwood. Later, ebony and cocuswood, exotic, dense products of the tropics, were widely adopted. Often trimmed with gold or silver, wooden flutes were prized examples of craftsmanship. More showy, but less practical, were flutes made of ivory or even glass. These were valued more as show pieces or curiosities than as serious instruments.

The metal flute is a product of the nineteenth century, when techniques and tools combined with new musical standards to encourage the use of silver and, occasionally, gold. The gold instrument of Mozart's *The Magic Flute* would have been unusual indeed when the opera was written at the end of the eighteenth century, but a hundred years later it seemed much more natural, especially for musicians seeking a

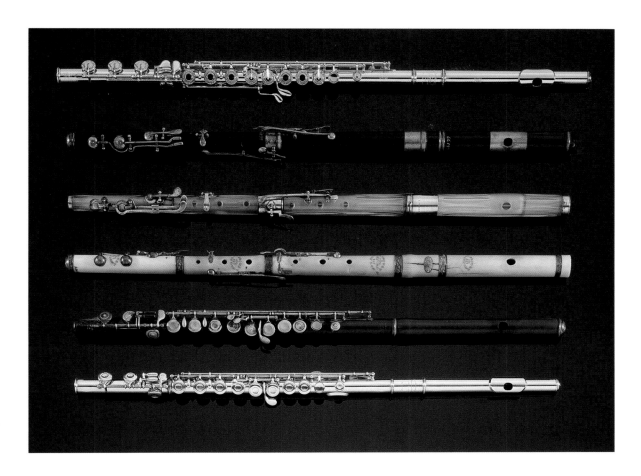

"warmer" tone than that of the more common silver. Platinum and gold together make an even more spectacular flute, though the musical advantages are less clear. By the end of the nineteenth century experiments on even more novel materials had made the flute of hard rubber practical, particularly when metal was used for certain parts. Such a flute was intended to offer the student or amateur an inexpensive yet suitable alternative to the precious metals and woods.

Top to bottom:

Platinum and Gold

These precious metals make fine materials for flutes, with distinctive tonal differences from the more common silver (although the platinum may be more for show).

Cocuswood and Silver

This was one of a number of exotic woods popular with European craftsmen in the nineteenth century. Like ebony, cocuswood was evidence of the widespread popularity of colonial products over native ones in the period of great overseas empires.

Glass

Glass flutes were often novelty pieces, experimented with for tonal effects and valued for their unusual appearance. They were difficult to make and very fragile.

Ivory

An ivory flute was generally not practical but was valued for showing the fine taste and wealth of the owner.

Ebonite (hard rubber) and Nickel-Silver

Rubber provided a cheaper material, to be used by students or others unable to afford silver (or other precious substances).

Silver

Since the nineteenth century, this has been the most widely used material for serious, orchestra-quality instruments, combining volume and clear tone.

Bicycles

Like all other vehicles in the early nineteenth century, the first bicycles were largely wooden. The wheels, the seat, and much of the frame were generally wood, and builders added a little iron or brass here and there for extra strength. Like everything from ships to railway cars, bicycles became more and more metallic as the century wore on. This was in part the result of tremendous growth in the iron and steel industry. But it was also a product of the perception of metals as the materials of progress and longevity and of the reality of nineteenth-century factory production, geared increasingly to machines and methods that favored iron and steel.

In the twentieth century the form of the bicycle has changed little, though the materials that go into it have grown steadily more sophisticated.

Counterclockwise from top left:

Laubach Velocipede, 1869

The earliest bicycles were made either of wood or iron, and the materials in this device were typical (even if the design was not—notice the "two-wheel steering" mechanism). The frame consists of iron rods, held together by bronze pieces; the wheels are wood with iron strips for tires [check]; the pedals are bronze; the wooden seat is made slightly more tolerable by a steel spring.

Starley Psycho is metal tubing, the handlebars are metal with wooden grips, and the saddle is leather. This bicycle also shows an early version of the thin rubber tires now common on bicycles. The manufacturers of this machine were awarded a gold medal at the International Exhibition at Toulouse, France, in 1887.

Whalen and Janssen, 1942

The steel-tube bicycle frame has been standard throughout the twentieth century, but sometimes special conditions prompted experiments with other materials. The use of laminated-wood in the frame of this bicycle helped to conserve strategically important steel during World War II. Not surprisingly, one of the makers was a piano manufacturer.

Razors

Few implements of daily life have changed so profoundly in the last century as the razor. In the nineteenth century the availability of good cast steel and the new technique of hollow-grinding blades produced an instrument that could take and maintain a sharp edge even in the hands of an unskilled grinder. In the course of the century the razor thus changed from a craftsman's instrument to a tool for everyman. Because the razor was seen as an intimate thing, associated with one of manhood's distinctive rituals, manufacturers still treated it with flair and style, sometimes by etching the blade but more often by using attractive materials for the handle.

The safety razor was introduced in the

Customized Columbia, 1896

Sometimes the machine look was not particularly desirable, as in the case of a fine lady's cycle. The nickel plating on the steel tubing of this bicycle, along with the gold plating and other ornamentation, is an effort to make it complement the other fine possessions of the southern gentlelady who rode it. The rubber pneumatic tires were another material improvement to bicycles in the 1890s.

Starley Psycho Safety Bicycle, about 1887

Like most other vehicles, bicycles became more metallic towards the end of the nineteenth century. The frame of the

late nineteenth century, initially as a way to make shaving a bit less hazardous to the sensitive or the clumsy. When traveling salesman and amateur political philosopher King C. Gillette combined the safety guard with the idea of cheap, disposable blades, a new industry was born and along with it a new way of thinking about razors and shaving. The technical key to Gillette's success was the thinness of the steel blades. He used so little material that once production techniques were worked out the blades would be cheap enough to throw away after only a week or so of use. At first the blade holder was treated with some of the same regard as the traditional razor, and embellished with attractive materials and some ornamentation. But gradually in our own century cheaper materials have displaced finer ones so that cheap disposability extends now to the entire instrument, and shaving has been reduced to a chore rather than a ritual.

Left to right:
Straight Razors
    Whalebone, French (decorated like scrimshaw)
    Brass
    Mother-of-pearl with silver inlay

Center row, left to right:
Safety Razors
    Plastic ("Featherweight") with gold metal trim
    Sterling silver (Gillette)
    Celluloid (Gem Junior Bar)
    Brass
    Plastic (Schick injector)

Bottom row, left to right:
    Plastic
    Plastic (disposable "Bic")

Revolvers

For at least two centuries before Samuel Colt's work in the 1830s, gunsmiths attempted to make a pistol with a revolving breech to hold and fire several shots before reloading. The revolver, however, was a great rarity until Colt and other inventors succeeded in designing and manufacturing the complex yet reliable mechanism of the modern weapon. As in all guns of the nineteenth century, the barrel and firing mechanisms of Colt's revolver are steel (although the fanciest guns could have an inlay or embossing of a decorative material like gold). Revolver grips have been made of a wide variety of materials, depending on the skill of the maker, the status and wealth of the owner, and the uses to which the weapon was to be put. As devices of power and authority, revolvers have often been carried primarily as symbols rather than practical tools, and so have incorporated exotic or expensive materials. Some gun owners also seek to associate themselves with a particular social class (from cowboys to country squires) or

historic periods or groups (from colonial days to Chicago gangsters) by the materials and designs of their revolver.

Top to bottom, left column:

Plastic

The plastic grip and chrome-plating of this .44 caliber Smith and Wesson are typical of today's handguns.

Hard rubber

The purchaser of a Colt "six-shooter" in the 1870s could have a hard-rubber grip instead of the ordinary walnut for a dollar extra. Such grips often had fancy patterns molded into them.

Center column:

Silver and gold plate

The plating and the elaborate engravings of this early twentieth-century Colt revolver suggest that it was meant primarily as a presentation piece rather than a weapon.

Ivory

In the mid-nineteenth century the purchaser of a Colt revolver could have an ivory grip for six dollars more than the regular price; for a little more money, he could have the ivory carved to order.

Aluminum with pearl inlay

The aluminum and mother-of-pearl grip of this Colt is not the original but rather an effort by an owner to dress up the gun with exotic materials.

Mother-of-pearl

The "Model 1" Smith and Wesson was the Colt's most important competitor. Dressed up in fancy materials such as mother-of-pearl, it was a particularly elegant weapon.

Right column:

Walnut

From the beginning black walnut was the material for the grip of the standard issue Colt revolver.

Imitation staghorn

This modern German weapon uses plastic to evoke the image of a gunslinger's revolver of the Wild West.

Bone

This turn-of-the-century Colt .38 was customized by its owner with a yellow bone grip.

Mortars and Pestles

The earliest mortar was a slightly hollowed stone in which a smaller stone was used to grind everything from grain to herbs. At least since the Middle Ages the mortar and pestle have taken on their distinctive shapes and have been made from a wide variety of materials. The wooden mortar was easy to shape and cheap to make, but it sometimes cracked and also tended to absorb some of the substances ground in it, especially if the mixture included a liquid. Some stones served well, but they also could absorb ground materials or liquids, broke or cracked easily (especially if heated), and were difficult to make or repair. Metal mortars were popular in the Renaissance and later; many were made of copper alloys, similar to those used for bells. Cast iron was a cheaper substitute, but all metal tended to tarnish and corrode over time. Glass or glazed ceramic mortars had the advantages of purity and imperviousness, though their fragility was sometimes a drawback. No material ultimately emerged as perfect for all uses, and for centuries it has been common for the well-stocked apothecary to keep a variety of mortars and pestles on hand.

wood (lignum vitae)	porcelain
cast iron	marble
glass	bell metal
alabaster	brass
agate	lava stone

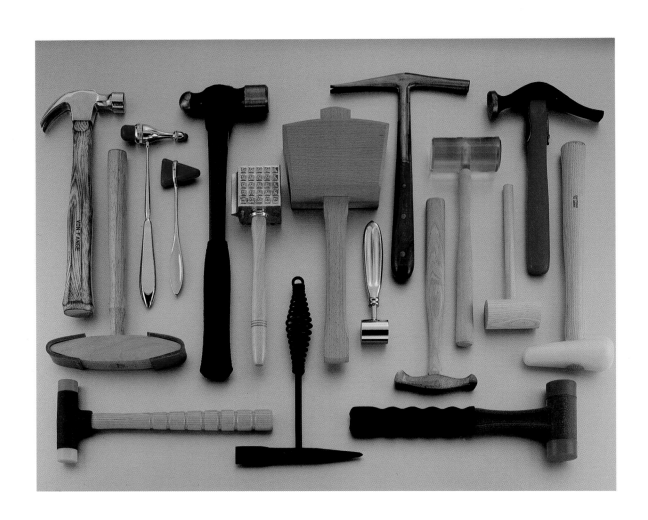

Hammers

No tool could be simpler than a hammer, but the variety of tasks to which hammers are put has yielded a bewildering number of sizes, forms, and materials for pounding, tapping, breaking, denting, sounding, and chasing.

Top row, left to right:

The copper-beryllium head of this cabinetmaker's hammer is chip-resistant, non-sparking, and very hard.

The leather covering the head of a silversmith's touch-up hammer allows for gentle final shaping.

Rubber on the end of the neurologist's hammer makes it possible to test nerve responses without damaging a patient's skin.

The familiar physician's reflex hammer has a rubber head for the same reason, while chromium-plated steel provides clean, corrosion-resistant handles.

The fiberglass and rubber in the handle of this hammer absorb the shock of striking against metal.

In a hammer where strength is no consideration, such as a chef's meat tenderizer, an aluminum head makes for light weight

Beech is a traditional material for the woodworker's chiseling mallet.

Brass and steel in the head of the surgeon's bone-breaking mallet give considerable heft to a necessarily small instrument.

The shock-absorbing qualities of hickory make it a favorite wood for many American hammers, like this one used for taking down carpets.

The silversmith's forming hammer also has a hickory handle.

The hickory handle in this craftsman's hammer is unremarkable, but the acetate head makes it ideal for uses where marring must be avoided.

Low cost but sturdy and clean-looking woods like ash and birch are used in the crab-cracking mallet.

The oak in this German shoemaker's hammer betrays its European source.

Relatively soft woods make this embossing mallet suitable for work on fine silver.

Bottom row, left and right:

Advanced plastics and steel are combined in the heads of these machinist's hammers.

Center:

The welder's chipping hammer is made completely of steel, for sturdiness and simplicity, not for heavy blows.

These nineteenth-century blacksmith's tools represent the traditional forms and uses of iron.

To Explore Further

Pauline G. Beery. *Stuff: The Story of Materials in the Service of Man.*
New York: D. Appleton and Company, 1930.

Rodney Cotterill. *The Cambridge Guide to the Material World.*
New York: Cambridge University Press, 1985.

Robert Friedel. *Pioneer Plastic: The Making and Selling of Celluloid.*
Madison: University of Wisconsin Press, 1983.

J. E. Gordon. *The New Science of Strong Materials, or Why You Don't Fall Through the Floor.*
Princeton, N.J.: Princeton University Press, 1976.

Williams Haynes. *This Chemical Age: The Miracle of Man-Made Materials.*
New York: Alfred A. Knopf, 1942.

Brooke Hindle, ed. *America's Wooden Age: Aspects of Its Early Technology.*
Tarrytown, N.Y.: Sleepy Hollow Press, 1975.

Peter J. T. Morris. *Polymer Pioneers.*
Philadelphia: Center for History of Chemistry (Publ. No. 5), 1986.

James Mulholland. *A History of Metals in Colonial America.*
University: University of Alabama Press, 1981.

Robert Raymond. *Out of the Fiery Furnace: The Impact of Metals on the History of Mankind.*
University Park: Pennsylvania State University Press, 1986.

Cyril Stanley Smith. *A Search for Structure: Selected Essays on Science, Art, and History.*
Cambridge, Mass.: MIT Press, 1981.

Typeset by Monotype Composition Company, Inc., Baltimore
Printed by Schneidereith and Sons, Inc., Baltimore
Designed by John Michael, Rockville, Maryland